Historia histrionica an historical account of the English stage, shewing the ancient use, improvement and perfection of dramatick representations in this nation in a dialogue of plays and players. (1699)

James Wright

Historia histrionica an historical account of the English stage, shewing the ancient use, improvement and perfection of dramatick representations in this nation in a dialogue of plays and players.
Wright, James, 1643-1713.
Caption title: A dialogue of plays and players.
[4], 32 p.
London : Printed by G. Croom for William Haws, 1699.
Wing / W3695
English
Reproduction of the original in the Henry E. Huntington Library and Art Gallery

Early English Books Online (EEBO) Editions

Imagine holding history in your hands.

Now you can. Digitally preserved and previously accessible only through libraries as Early English Books Online, this rare material is now available in single print editions. Thousands of books written between 1475 and 1700 and ranging from religion to astronomy, medicine to music, can be delivered to your doorstep in individual volumes of high-quality historical reproductions.

We have been compiling these historic treasures for more than 70 years. Long before such a thing as "digital" even existed, ProQuest founder Eugene Power began the noble task of preserving the British Museum's collection on microfilm. He then sought out other rare and endangered titles, providing unparalleled access to these works and collaborating with the world's top academic institutions to make them widely available for the first time. This project furthers that original vision.

These texts have now made the full journey -- from their original printing-press versions available only in rare-book rooms to online library access to new single volumes made possible by the partnership between artifact preservation and modern printing technology. A portion of the proceeds from every book sold supports the libraries and institutions that made this collection possible, and that still work to preserve these invaluable treasures passed down through time.

This is history, traveling through time since the dawn of printing to your own personal library.

Initial Proquest EEBO Print Editions collections include:

Early Literature

This comprehensive collection begins with the famous Elizabethan Era that saw such literary giants as Chaucer, Shakespeare and Marlowe, as well as the introduction of the sonnet. Traveling through Jacobean and Restoration literature, the highlight of this series is the Pollard and Redgrave 1475-1640 selection of the rarest works from the English Renaissance.

Early Documents of World History

This collection combines early English perspectives on world history with documentation of Parliament records, royal decrees and military documents that reveal the delicate balance of Church and State in early English government. For social historians, almanacs and calendars offer insight into daily life of common citizens. This exhaustively complete series presents a thorough picture of history through the English Civil War.

Historical Almanacs

Historically, almanacs served a variety of purposes from the more practical, such as planting and harvesting crops and plotting nautical routes, to predicting the future through the movements of the stars. This collection provides a wide range of consecutive years of "almanacks" and calendars that depict a vast array of everyday life as it was several hundred years ago.

Early History of Astronomy & Space

Humankind has studied the skies for centuries, seeking to find our place in the universe. Some of the most important discoveries in the field of astronomy were made in these texts recorded by ancient stargazers, but almost as impactful were the perspectives of those who considered their discoveries to be heresy. Any independent astronomer will find this an invaluable collection of titles arguing the truth of the cosmic system.

Early History of Industry & Science

Acting as a kind of historical Wall Street, this collection of industry manuals and records explores the thriving industries of construction; textile, especially wool and linen; salt; livestock; and many more.

Early English Wit, Poetry & Satire

The power of literary device was never more in its prime than during this period of history, where a wide array of political and religious satire mocked the status quo and poetry called humankind to transcend the rigors of daily life through love, God or principle. This series comments on historical patterns of the human condition that are still visible today.

Early English Drama & Theatre

This collection needs no introduction, combining the works of some of the greatest canonical writers of all time, including many plays composed for royalty such as Queen Elizabeth I and King Edward VI. In addition, this series includes history and criticism of drama, as well as examinations of technique.

Early History of Travel & Geography

Offering a fascinating view into the perception of the world during the sixteenth and seventeenth centuries, this collection includes accounts of Columbus's discovery of the Americas and encompasses most of the Age of Discovery, during which Europeans and their descendants intensively explored and mapped the world. This series is a wealth of information from some the most groundbreaking explorers.

Early Fables & Fairy Tales

This series includes many translations, some illustrated, of some of the most well-known mythologies of today, including Aesop's Fables and English fairy tales, as well as many Greek, Latin and even Oriental parables and criticism and interpretation on the subject.

Early Documents of Language & Linguistics

The evolution of English and foreign languages is documented in these original texts studying and recording early philology from the study of a variety of languages including Greek, Latin and Chinese, as well as multilingual volumes, to current slang and obscure words. Translations from Latin, Hebrew and Aramaic, grammar treatises and even dictionaries and guides to translation make this collection rich in cultures from around the world.

Early History of the Law

With extensive collections of land tenure and business law "forms" in Great Britain, this is a comprehensive resource for all kinds of early English legal precedents from feudal to constitutional law, Jewish and Jesuit law, laws about public finance to food supply and forestry, and even "immoral conditions." An abundance of law dictionaries, philosophy and history and criticism completes this series.

Early History of Kings, Queens and Royalty

This collection includes debates on the divine right of kings, royal statutes and proclamations, and political ballads and songs as related to a number of English kings and queens, with notable concentrations on foreign rulers King Louis IX and King Louis XIV of France, and King Philip II of Spain. Writings on ancient rulers and royal tradition focus on Scottish and Roman kings, Cleopatra and the Biblical kings Nebuchadnezzar and Solomon.

Early History of Love, Marriage & Sex

Human relationships intrigued and baffled thinkers and writers well before the postmodern age of psychology and self-help. Now readers can access the insights and intricacies of Anglo-Saxon interactions in sex and love, marriage and politics, and the truth that lies somewhere in between action and thought.

Early History of Medicine, Health & Disease

This series includes fascinating studies on the human brain from as early as the 16th century, as well as early studies on the physiological effects of tobacco use. Anatomy texts, medical treatises and wound treatment are also discussed, revealing the exponential development of medical theory and practice over more than two hundred years.

Early History of Logic, Science and Math

The "hard sciences" developed exponentially during the 16th and 17th centuries, both relying upon centuries of tradition and adding to the foundation of modern application, as is evidenced by this extensive collection. This is a rich collection of practical mathematics as applied to business, carpentry and geography as well as explorations of mathematical instruments and arithmetic; logic and logicians such as Aristotle and Socrates; and a number of scientific disciplines from natural history to physics.

Early History of Military, War and Weaponry

Any professional or amateur student of war will thrill at the untold riches in this collection of war theory and practice in the early Western World. The Age of Discovery and Enlightenment was also a time of great political and religious unrest, revealed in accounts of conflicts such as the Wars of the Roses.

Early History of Food

This collection combines the commercial aspects of food handling, preservation and supply to the more specific aspects of canning and preserving, meat carving, brewing beer and even candy-making with fruits and flowers, with a large resource of cookery and recipe books. Not to be forgotten is a "the great eater of Kent," a study in food habits.

Early History of Religion

From the beginning of recorded history we have looked to the heavens for inspiration and guidance. In these early religious documents, sermons, and pamphlets, we see the spiritual impact on the lives of both royalty and the commoner. We also get insights into a clergy that was growing ever more powerful as a political force. This is one of the world's largest collections of religious works of this type, revealing much about our interpretation of the modern church and spirituality.

Early Social Customs

Social customs, human interaction and leisure are the driving force of any culture. These unique and quirky works give us a glimpse of interesting aspects of day-to-day life as it existed in an earlier time. With books on games, sports, traditions, festivals, and hobbies it is one of the most fascinating collections in the series.

old books. new life.

The BiblioLife Network

This project was made possible in part by the BiblioLife Network (BLN), a project aimed at addressing some of the huge challenges facing book preservationists around the world. The BLN includes libraries, library networks, archives, subject matter experts, online communities and library service providers. We believe every book ever published should be available as a high-quality print reproduction; printed on-demand anywhere in the world. This insures the ongoing accessibility of the content and helps generate sustainable revenue for the libraries and organizations that work to preserve these important materials.

The following book is in the "public domain" and represents an authentic reproduction of the text as printed by the original publisher. While we have attempted to accurately maintain the integrity of the original work, there are sometimes problems with the original work or the micro-film from which the books were digitized. This can result in minor errors in reproduction. Possible imperfections include missing and blurred pages, poor pictures, markings and other reproduction issues beyond our control. Because this work is culturally important, we have made it available as part of our commitment to protecting, preserving, and promoting the world's literature.

GUIDE TO FOLD-OUTS MAPS and OVERSIZED IMAGES

The book you are reading was digitized from microfilm captured over the past thirty to forty years. Years after the creation of the original microfilm, the book was converted to digital files and made available in an online database.

In an online database, page images do not need to conform to the size restrictions found in a printed book. When converting these images back into a printed bound book, the page sizes are standardized in ways that maintain the detail of the original. For large images, such as fold-out maps, the original page image is split into two or more pages

Guidelines used to determine how to split the page image follows:

• Some images are split vertically; large images require vertical and horizontal splits.
• For horizontal splits, the content is split left to right.
• For vertical splits, the content is split from top to bottom.
• For both vertical and horizontal splits, the image is processed from top left to bottom right.

INCHES

XEROX MICROFORMS SYSTEMS
University Microfilms

(313) 761-4700

Ann Arbor, Michigan 48106

METRIC

HISTORIA HISTRIONICA:

AN

Hiftorical Account

OF THE

English-Stage,

SHEWING

The ancient Ufe, Improvement, and Perfection, of Dramatick Reprefentations, in this Nation.

IN A

Dialogue, of *PLAYS* and *PLAYERS*.

------ *Olim meminiffe juvabit.*

LONDON.

Printed by G. *Croom,* for *William Haws* at the Rofe in *Ludgate-ftreet.* 1699.

THE
PREFACE.

MUch has been Writ of late pro and con, about the Stage, yet the Subject admits of more, and that which has not been hetherto toucht upon; not only what that is, but what it was, about which some People have made such a Busle. What it is we see, and I think it has been sufficiently display'd in Mr. Colier's Book; What it was in former Ages, and how used in this Kingdom, so far back as one may collect any Memorialls, is the Subject of the follow-

ing

The PREFACE.

ing Dialogue. Old Plays will be always Read by the Curious, if it were only to difcover the Manners and Behaviour of feveral Ages; and how they alter'd. For Plays are exactly like Portraits Drawn in the Garb and Fafhion of the time when Painted. You fee one Habit in the time of King Charles I. another quite different from that, both for Men and Women, in Queen Elizabeths time, another; under Henry the Eighth different from both; and fo backward all various. And in the feveral Fafhions of Behaviour and Converfation, there is as much Matability as in that of Cloaths. Religion and Religious matters was once as much the Mode in publick Entertainments, as the Contrary has been

in

in some times since. This appears
in the different Plays of several Ages:
And to evince this, the following
Sheets are an Essay or Specimen.

Some may think the Subject of this
Discourse trivial, and the persons
herein mention'd not worth remember-
ing. But besides that I could name
some things contested of late with
great heat, of as little, or less Conse-
quence, the Reader may know that
the Profession of Players is not so
totally scandalous, nor all of them so
reprobate, but that there has been
found under that Name, a Canonized
Saint in the primitive Church; as
may be seen in the Roman Martyrology on the 29th of March; his
name Masculas a Master of Interludes, (the Latin is Archimimus,
and

The PREFACE.

and the French Translation un Mai-
tre Comedien) *who under the Per-
secution of the* Vandals *in* Africa,
by Geisericus *the Arian King, having endured many and greivious Tor-
ments and Reproaches for the Con-
fession of the Truth, finisht the Course
of this glorious Combat.* Saith the
said Martyrology.

*It appears from this, and some
further Instances in the following Discourse, That there have been* Players
*of worthy Principles as to Religion,
Loyalty, and other Virtues; and if the
major part of them fall under a different Character, it is the general un-
happiness of* Mankind, *that the* Most
are the Worst.

A

A DIALOGUE

OF

PLAYS and *PLAYERS*.

Lovewit, Truman.

Lovew. Honeſt Old Cavalier! well met, 'faith I'm glad to ſee thee.

Trum. Have a care what you call me. Old, is a Word of Diſgrace among the Ladies; to be Honeſt is to be Poor and Fooliſh, (as ſome think) and Cavalier is a Word as much out of Faſhion as any of 'em.

Lovew. The more's the pity: But what ſaid the Fortune-Teller in *Ben. Johnſon's* Maſk of *Gypſies,* to the then *Lord Privy Seal,*

Honeſt and Old!
In thoſe the Good Part of a Fortune is told.

B   *Trum.*

Trum. *Ben. Johnson?* How dare you name *Ben. Johnson* in thefe times? When we have fuch a crowd of Poets of a quite different Genius; the leaft of which thinks himfelf as well able to correct *Ben. Johnson,* as he could a Country School Miftrefs that taught to Spell.

Lovew. We have indeed, Poets of a different Genius; fo are the Plays: But in my Opinion, they are all of 'em (fome few excepted) as much inferior to thofe of former Times, as the Actors now in being (generally fpeaking) are, compared to *Hart, Mohun, Burt, Lacy, Clun,* and *Shatterel;* for I can reach no farther backward.

Trum. I can; and dare affure you, if my Fancy and Memory are not partial (for Men of my Age are apt to be over indulgent to the thoughts of their youthful Days) I fay the Actors that I have feen before the Wars, *Lowin, Tayler, Pollard,* and fome others, were almoft as far beyond *Hart* and his Company, as thofe were beyond thefe now in being.

Lovew. I am willing to believe it, but cannot readily; becaufe I have been told, That thofe whom I mention'd, were Bred up under the others of your Acquaintance, and follow'd their manner of Action, which is now loft. So far, that when the Queftion has been askt, Why thefe Players do not receive the *Silent Woman,* and fome other of *Johnson's* Plays, (once of higheft efteem) they have anfwer'd, truly, Becaufe there are none now Living who can rightly

rightly Humour thofe Parts, for all who related to the *Black-friers* (where they were
Acted in perfection) are now Dead, and almoft forgotten.

Trum. 'Tis very true, *Hart* and *Clun*, were
bred up Boys at the *Blackfriers*; and Acted
Womens Parts, *Hart* was *Robinfon*'s Boy or
Apprentice: He Acted the Dutchefs in the
Tragedy of *the Cardinal*, which was the firft
Part that gave him Reputation. *Cartwright*,
and *Winterfhal* belong'd to the private Houfe
in *Salisbury-Court*, *Burt* was a Boy firft under
Shank at the *Black-friers*, then under *Beefton* at
the *Cockpit*; and *Mohun*, and *Shatterel* were
in the fame Condition with him, at the laft
Place. There *Burt* ufed to Play the principal
Women's Parts, in particular *Clariana* in *Love's
Cruelty*; and at the fame time *Mohun* Acted *Bella-
mente*, which Part he retain'd after the Reftau-
ration.

Lovew. That I have feen, and can well remember. I wifh they had Printed in the laft
Age (fo I call the times before the Rebellion)
the Actors Names over againft the Parts they
Acted, as they have done fince the Reftaurati-
on. And thus one might have gueft at the
Action of the Men, by the Parts which we
now Read in the Old Plays.

Trum. It was not the Cuftome and Ufage
of thofe Days, as it hath been fince. Yet
fome few Old Plays there are that have the
Names fet againft the Parts, as, *The Dutchefs*

of

of Malfy ..... *Picture*; the *Roman Actor*; the deferving Favourite, the *Wild Goofe Chace*, (at the Black-friers) the *Wedding*; the *Renegado*; the fair *Maid* of the *VVeft*; *Hannibal and Scipio*; *King John and Matilda*; (at the Cockpit) and *Holland's Leaguer*, (at Salisbury Court.)

Lovew. Thefe are but few indeed: But pray Sir, what Mafter Parts can you remember the Old *Black-friers* Men to Act, in *Johnfon*, *Shakefpear*, and *Fletcher's* Plays.

Trum. What I can at prefent recollect I'll tell you; *Shakefpear*, (who as I have heard, was a much better Poet, than Player) *Burbadge*, *Hemmings*, and others of the Older fort, were Dead before I knew the Town; but in my time, before the Wars, *Lowin* ufed to Act, with mighty Applaufe, *Falftaffe*, *Morofe*, *Vulpone*, and *Mammon* in the *Alchymift*; *Melantius* in the *Maid's* Tragedy, and at the fame time *Amyntor* was Play'd by *Stephen Hammerton*, (who was at firft a moft noted and beautiful Woman Actor, but afterwards he acted with equal Grace and Applaufe, a Young Lover's Part) *Tayler* Acted *Hamlet* incomparably well, *Jago*, *Truewit* in the *Silent Woman*, and *Face* in the *Alchymift*; *Swanfton* ufed to Play *Othello*: *Pollard*, and *Robinfon* were Comedians, fo was *Shank* who ufed to Act Sir *Roger*, in the *Scornful Lady*. Thefe were of the *Black-friers*. Thofe of principal Note at the *Cockpit*, were, *Perkins*, *Michael Bowyer*, *Sumner*, *William Allen*, and *Bird*, eminent Actors. and *Robins*, *bles* a Comedian. Of the other Companies I took little notice.

Lovew. Were there fo many Companies?

Trum. Before the Wars, there were in being all thefe Play-houfes at the fame time. The *Black-friers*, and *Globe* on the *Bankfide*, a Winter and Summer Houfe, belonging to the fame Company called the King's Servants; the *Cockpit* or *Phænix*, in *Drury-lane*, called the Queen's Servants; the private Houfe in *Salisbury court*, called the Prince's Servants; the *Fortune* near *White-crofs-ftreet*, and the *Red Bull* at the upper end of St. *John's-ftreet*: The two laft were moftly frequented by Citizens, and the meaner fort of People. All thefe Companies got Money, and Liv'd in Reputation, efpecially thofe of the *Blackfriers*, who were Men of grave and fober Behaviour.

Lovew. Which I admire at; That the Town much lefs than at prefent, could then maintain Five Companies, and yet now Two can hardly Subfift.

Trum. Do not wonder, but confider, That tho' the Town was then, perhaps, not much more than half fo Populous as now, yet then the Prices were fmall (there being no Scenes) and better order kept among the Company that came; which made very good People think a Play an Innocent Diverfion for an idle Hour or two, the Plays themfelves being then, for the moft part, more Inftructive and Moral. Whereas of late, the Play-houfes are fo extreamly

peftered

peftered with Vizard-masks and their 'Trade, (occafioning continual Quarrels and Abufes) that many of the more Civilized Part of the Town are uneafy in the Company, and fhun the Theater as they would a Houfe of Scandal. It is an Argument of the worth of the Plays and Actors, of the laft Age, and eafily inferr'd, that they were much beyond ours in this, to confider that they cou'd fupport themfelves meerly from their own Merit ; the weight of the Matter, and goodnefs of the Action, without Scenes and Machines: Whereas the prefent Plays with all that fhew, can hardly draw an Audience, unlefs there be the additional Invitation of a *Signior Fideli*, a *Monfieur L'abbe*, or fome fuch Foreign Regale expreft in the bottom of the Bill.

Lovew. To wave this Digreffion, I have Read of one *Edward Allin*, a Man fo famed for excellent Action, that among *Ben. Johnfon's* Epigrams, I find one directed to him, full of Encomium, and concluding thus

Wear his Renown, 'tis juft that who did give
So many Poets Life, by one fhould Live.

Was he one of the *Black-friers* ?
Trum. Never, as I have heard ; (for he was Dead before my time.) He was Mafter of a Company of his own, for whom he Built the *Fortune* Play-houfe from the Ground, a large, round Brick Building. This is he that grew fo

Rich

Rich that he purchaſed a great Eſtate in *Surrey* and elſewhere; and having no Iſſue, he Built and largely endow'd *Dulwich* College, in the Year 1619, for a Maſter, a Warden, Four Fellows, Twelve aged poor People, and Twelve poor Boys, *&c.* A noble Charity.

Lovew. What kind of Playhouſes had they before the Wars?

Trum. The *Black-friers*, *Cockpit*, and *Salisbury-court*, were called Private Houſes, and were very ſmall to what we ſee now. The *Cockpit* was ſtanding ſince the Reſtauration, and *Rhode*'s Company Acted there for ſome time.

Lovew. I have ſeen that.

Trum. Then you have ſeen the other two, in effect; for they were all three Built almoſt exactly alike, for Form and Bigneſs. Here they had Pits for the Gentry, and Acted by Candle-light. The *Globe*, *Fortune* and *Bull*, were large Houſes, and lay partly open to the Weather, and there they alwaies Acted by Daylight.

Lovew. But prithee, *Truman*, what became of theſe Players when the Stage was put down, and the Rebellion raiſed?

Trum. Moſt of 'em, except *Lowin*, *Tayler* and *Pollard*, (who were ſuperannuated) went into the King's Army, and like good Men and true, Serv'd their Old Maſter, tho' in a different, yet more honourable, Capacity. *Robinſon* was Kill'd at the Taking of a Place (I

think

think *Basing House*) by *Harrison*, he that was
after Hang'd at *Charing-crofs*, who refufed
him Quarter, and Shot him in the Head when
he had laid down his Arms; abufing Scrip-
ture at the fame time, in faying, *Curfed is he
that doth the Work of the Lord negligently.*
Mohun was a Captain, (and after the Wars
were ended here, ferved in *Flanders*, where he
received Pay as a Major) *Hart* was a Lieute-
nant of Horfe under Sir *Thomas Dallifon*, in
Prince Rupert's, Regiment, *Burt* was Cornet in
the fame Troop, and *Shatterel* Quarter-maf-
ter. *Allen* of the *Cockpit*, was a Major, and Quarter Mafter General at *Oxford*. I have not heard
of one of thefe Players of any Note that fided
with the other Party, but only *Swanfton*, and
he profeft himfelf a Presbyterian, took up the
Trade of a Jeweller, and liv'd in *Alderman-
bury*, within the Territory of Father *Calamy*.
The reft either Loft, or expos'd their Lives
for their King. When the Wars were over,
and the Royalifts totally Subdued; moft of
'em who were left alive gather'd to *London*,
and for a Subfiftence endeavour'd to revive
their Old Trade, privately. They made up
one Company out of all the Scatter'd Members of Several; and in the Winter before
the King's Murder, 1648, They ventured to
Act fome Plays with as much caution and
privacy as cou'd be, at the *Cockpit*. They con-
tinu'd undifturbed for three or four Days;
but at laft as they were prefenting the Tragedy

gedy of the *Bloudy Brother*, (in which *Lowin* Acted Aubrey, *Tayler* Rollo, *Pollard* the Cook, *Burt* Latorch, and I think *Hart* Otto) a Party of Foot Souldiers befet the Houfe, furprized 'em about the midle of the Play, and carried 'em away in their habits, not admitting them to Shift, to *Hatton-houfe* then a Prifon, where having detain'd them fometime, they Plunder'd them of their Cloths and let 'em loofe again. Afterwards in *Oliver*'s time, they ufed to Act privately, three or four Miles, or more, out of Town, now here, now there, fometimes in Noblemens Houfes, in particular *Holland-houfe* at *Kenfington*, where the Nobility and Gentry who met (but in no great Numbers) ufed to make a Sum for them, each giving a broad Peice, or the like. And *Alexander Goffe*, the Woman Actor at *Blackfriers*, (who had made himfelf known to Perfons of Quality) ufed to be the Jackal and give notice of Time and Place. At Chriftmafs, and Bartlemew-fair, they ufed to Bribe the Officer who Commanded the Guard at *Whitehall*, and were thereupon connived at to Act for a few Days, at the *Red Bull*; but were fometimes notwithftanding Difturb'd by Soldiers. Some pickt up a little Money by publifhing the Copies of Plays never before Printed, but kept up in Manufcript. For inftance, in the Year 1652, *Beaumont* and *Fletcher's Wild Goofe Chace* was Printed in Folio, *for the Publick ufe of all the Ingenious*, (as the Title-

C.   page

page (says) *and private Benefit of* John Lowin *and* Joseph Tayler, *Servants to his late Majesty*; and by them Dedicated *To the Honour'd few Lovers of Dramatick Poesy* : Wherein they modestly intimate their Wants. And that with sufficient Cause; for whatever they were before the Wars, they were, after, reduced to a necessitous Condition. *Lowin* in his latter Days, kept an Inn (the three Pidgions) at *Brentford,* where he Dyed very Old, (for he was an Actor of eminent Note in the Reign of K. *James* the first) and his Poverty was as great as his Age. *Tayler* Dyed at *Richmond* and was there Buried. *Pollard* who Lived Single, and had a Competent Estate; Retired to some Relations he had in the Country, and there ended his Life. *Perkins* and *Sumner* of the *Cockpit,* kept House together at *Clerkenwel,* and were there Buried. These all Dyed some Years before the Restauration. What follow'd after, I need not tell you: You can easily Remember.

Lovew. Yes, presently after the Restauration, the King's Players Acted publickly at the *Red Bull* for some time, and then Removed to a New-built Playhouse in *Vere-street* by *Claremarket.* There they continued for a Year or two, and then removed to the *Theater Royal* in *Drury-lane,* where they first made use of Scenes, which had been a little before introduced upon the publick Stage by Sir *William Davenant* at the *Duke's Old Theater* in

Lin-

Lincolns-Inn-fields, but afterwards very much improved, with the Addition of curious Machines by Mr. *Betterton* at the New Theater in *Dorfet-Garden*, to the great Expence and continual Charge of the Players. This much impair'd their Profit o'er what it was before; for I have been inform'd, (by one of 'em) That for *feveral Years next after the Reftaur-ation*, every whole Sharer in Mr. *Hart*'s Company, got 1000 *l. per an*. About the fame time that Scenes firft enter'd upon the Stage at *London*, Women were taught to Act their own Parts; fince when, we have feen at both Houfes feveral excellent Actreffes, juftly famed as well for Beauty, as perfect good Action. And fome Plays (in particular *The Parfon's Wedding*) have been Prefented all by Women, as formerly all by Men. Thus it continued for about 20 Years, when Mr. *Hart* and fome of the Old Men began to grow weary, and were minded to leave off; then the two Companies thought fit to Unite; but of late, you fee, they have thought it no lefs fit to Divide again, though both Companies keep the fame Name of his Majefty's Servants. All this while the Play-houfe Mufick improved Yearly, and is now arrived to greater Perfection than ever I knew it. Yet for all thefe Advantages, the Reputation of the Stage, and Peoples Affection to it, are much Decay'd, Some were lately fevere againft it, and would

C 2   hardly

hardly allow Stage-Plays fit to be longer permitted. Have you feen Mr. *Collier*'s Book?

Trum. Yes, and his Oppofer's.

Lovew. And what think you?

Trum. In my mind Mr. *Collier*'s Reflections are Pertinent, and True, in the Main; the Book ingenioufly Writ, and well Intended: But he has overfhot himfelf in fome Places; and his Refpondents, perhaps, in more. My affection inclines me not to Engage on either fide, but rather Mediate. If there be Abufes relating to the Stage; (which I think is too apparent) Let the Abufe be reformed, and not the ufe, for that Reafon only, Abolifh'd. 'Twas an Old faying when I was a Boy,

Abfit Abufus non defit totaliter Vfus.

I fhall not run through Mr. *Collier's* Book; I will only touch a little on two or three general Notions, in which, I think he may be miftaken. What he urges out of the Primitive Councils, and Fathers of the Church, feems to me to be directed againft the Heathen Plays, which were a fort of Religious Worfhip with them, to the Honour of *Ceres, Flora,* or fome of their falfe Deities; they had always a little Altar on their Stages, as appears plain enough from fome places in *Plautus*. And Mr. *Collier* himfelf p. 235. tells us out of *Livy,* that Plays were brought in upon the Score of

of Religion, to pacify the Gods. No wonder then, they forbid Chriftans to be prefent at them, for it was almoft the fame as to be prefent at their Sacrifices. We muft alfo ob-ferve that this was in the Infancy of Chrifti-anity, when the Church was under fevere, and almoft continual Perfecutions, and when all its true Members were of moft ftrict and exemplary Lives, not knowing when they fhould be call'd to the Stake, or thrown to Wild-Beafts. They communicated Daily, and expected Death hourly; their thoughts were intent upon the next World, they abftain'd al-moft wholy from all Diverfions and pleafures (though lawfull and Innocent) in this. Af-terwards when Perfecution ceafed, and the Church flourifht, Chriftians being then freed from their former Terrors, allow'd themfelves, at proper times, the lawfull Recreations of Converfation, and among other (no doubt) this of Shewes and Reprefentations. After this time, the Cenfures of the Church indeed, might be continued, or revived, upon occafion, againft Plays and Players, tho' (in my Opi-nion) it can not be underftood generally, but only againft fuch Players who were of Vicious and Licencious Lives, and reprefented profane Subjects, inconfiftant with the Morals and probity of Manners requifite to Chrifti-ans; and frequented chiefly by fuch loofe and Debaucht People as were much more apt to Corrupt than Divert thofe who affociated with
them

them. I say, I can not think the Canons and Censures of the Fathers can be applyed to all Players, *quatenus* Players; for if so how could Plays be continued among the Christians, as they were, of Divine Subjects, and Scriptural Stories? A late French Author Speaking of the Original of the *Hotel De Bourgogne* (a Play-house in *Paris*) says that the ancient Dukes of that Name gave it to the Brother-hood of the Passion, established in the Church of Trinity-Hospital in the *Rue* S. *Denis,* on condition that they should represent here Interludes of Devotion: And adds that there have been publick Shews in this Place 600 Years ago. The Spanish and Portuguize continue still to have, for the most part, such Ecclesiastical Stories, for the Subject of their Plays: And if we may beleive *Gage,* they are Acted in their Churches in *Mexico,* and the Spanish *West-Indies.*

Lovew. That's a great way off, *Truman*; I had rather you would come nearer Home, and confine your discourse to Old *England.*

Trum. So I intend. The same has been done here in *England*; for otherwise how comes it to be prohibited in the 88*th* Canon, among those past in Convocation, 1603. Certain it is that our ancient Plays were of Religious Subjects, and had for their Actors, (if not Priests) yet Men relating to the Church.

Lovew. How does that appear?

Trum.

Trum. Nothing clearer. *Stow* in his Survey of *London*, has one Chapter *of the Sports and Paſtimes of old time uſed in this City*, and there he tells us, That in the Year 1391 *(which was* 15 *R.* 2.*)* a Stage-Play was play'd by the Pariſh-Clerks of *London*, at the *Skinner's-well* beſide *Smithfield*, which Play continued three Days together, the King, Queen, and Nobles of the Realm being preſent. And another was play'd in the Year 1409 *(*11 *H.* 4.*)* which laſted eight Days, and was of Matter from the Creation of the World; whereat was preſent moſt part of the Nobility and Gentry of *England.* Sir *William Dugdale* in his Antiquities of *Warwickſhire*, p. 116, ſpeaking of the *Gray-Friers* (or *Franciſcans)* at *Coventry*, ſays, Before the ſuppreſſion of the Monaſteries, this City was very famous for the Pageants that were play'd therein upon *Corpus-Chriſti* Day; which Pageants being acted with mighty State and Reverence by the Friers of this Houſe, had Theatres for the ſeveral Scenes very large and high, plac'd upon Wheels, and drawn to all the eminent Parts of the City, for the better advantage of the Spectators; and contain'd the Story of the New Teſtament, compoſed in old Engliſh Rhime. An ancient Manuſcript of the ſame is now to be ſeen in the *Cottonian* Library, *Sub Effig. Veſpat. D.* 8. Since the Reformation, in Queen *Elizabeth*'s time, Plays were frequently acted by Quiriſters and Singing Boys; and ſeveral of our old Comedies have printed in the

Title

Title Page, *Acted by the Children of* Paul's, (not the School, but the Church) others, *By the Children of her Majesty's Chappel* ; in particular, *Cinthias Revels*, and the *Poetaster* were play'd by them ; who were at that time famous for good Action. Among *Ben. Johnson's* Epigrams you may find *An Epitaph on S. P.* (Sal. Pavy) *one of the Children of Queen* Elizabeth's *Chappel* ; part of which runs thus,

> *Years he counted scarce Thirteen*
> *When Fates turn'd Cruel,*
> *Yet three fill'd Zodiacks he had been*
> *The Stages-Jewell.*
> *And did act (what now we moan)*
> *Old Man so duly,*
> *As, sooth, the* Parcæ *thought him one,*
> *He play'd so truly.*

Some of these Chappel Boys, when they grew Men, became Actors at the *Black-friers* ; such were *Nathan Feild*, and *John Underwood.* Now I can hardly imagine that such Plays and Players as these, are included in the severe Censure of the Councils and Fathers ; but such only who are truly within the Character given by *Didacus de Tapia*, cited by Mr. *Collier*, p. 276, *viz. The infamous Playhouse ; a place of contradiction to the strictness and sobriety of Religion ; a place hated by God, and haunted by the Devil.* And for such I have as great an abhorrence as any Man.

Love-

Lovew. Can you guefs of what Antiquity the reprefenting of Religious Matters, on the Stage, hath been in *England?*

Trum. How long before the Conqueft I know not, but that it was ufed in *London* not long after, appears by *Fitz-Stevens,* an Author who wrote in the Reign of King *Henry* the Second. His Words are, *Londonia pro fpectaculis theatralibus, pro ludis fcenicis, ludos habet fanctiores, Reprefentationes miraculorum, qua fancti Confeffores operati funt, feu Reprefentationes paffionum quibus claruit conftantia Martyrum.* Of this, the Manufcript which I lately mention'd, in the *Cottonian* Library, is a notable inftance. Sir *William Dugdale* cites this Manufcript, by the Title of *Ludus Coventriæ*; but in the printed Catalogue of that Library, p. 113, it is named thus, *A Collection of Plays in old Englifh Metre.* h. e. *Dramata facra in quibus exhibentur hiftoriæ veteris & N. Teftamenti, introductis quafi in Scenam perfonis illic memoratis, quas fecum invicem colloquentes pro ingenio fingit Poeta. Videntur olim coram populo, five ad inftruendum five ad placendum, a fratibus mendicantibus repræfentata.* It appears by the latter end of the Prologue, that thefe Plays or Interludes, were not only play'd at *Coventry,* but in other Towns and Places upon occafion. And poffibly this may be the fame Play which *Stow* tells us was play'd in the Reign of King *Henry* IV, which lafted for Eight Days. The Book feems by the Character and Language to be at leaft 300 Years

old

old. It begins with a general Prologue, giving the Arguments of 40 Pageants or Gesticulations (which were as so many several Acts or Scenes) representing all the Histories of both Testaments from the Creation, to the choosing of St. *Mathias* to be an Apostle. The Stories of the New Testament are more largely exprest, *viz.* The Annunciation, Nativity, Visitation ; but more especially all Matters relating to the Passion very particularly, the Resurrection, Ascention, the choice of St. *Mathias* : After which is also represented the Assumption, and last Judgment. All these things were treated of in a very homely Style, (as we now think) infinitely below the Dignity of the Subject : But it seems the Gust of that Age was not so nice and delicate in these Matters ; the plain and incurious Judgment of our Ancestors, being prepared with favour, and taking every thing by the right and easiest Handle : For example, in the Scene relating to the Visitation.

Maria

But Husband of oo thyng pray you most mekely,
Are knowing that our Cosyn Elizabeth with childe is,
It it please you to go to her hastyly,
That we myth comfort her it mer to me blys.

Joseph.

I sake, is she with childe, sche ?
I her husband Zachary be mery.

In

In Montana they dwelle, fer hence, fo mote the,
In the City of Juda, I know it verily;
It is hence I trowe myles two a fifty,
We ar like to be wery or we come at the fame.
I wole with a good will, bleffyd wyff Mary;
Now go we forth then in goddys name, &c.

A little before the Refurrection.

Nunc dormient milites, & veniet anima Chrifti de inferno, cùm Adam *&* Eva, Abraham, John Baptift, *& alijs.*

Anima Chrifti.

Come forth Adam, and Eve with the,
And all my fryndes that herein be,
In Paradys come forth with me
   In blyffe for to dwelle.
The fende of hell that is yowr foo
He fhall be wrappyd and woundyn in woo:
Fro wo to welth now fhall ye go,
   With myrth euer mor to melle.

Adam.

I thank the Lord of thy grete grace
That now is forgiuen my gret trefpace,
Now fhall we dwellyn in blyffull pace, &c.

The laft Scene or Pageant, which reprefents the Day of Judgment, begins thus.

Michael.

Surgite, All men aryfe,
Venite ad judicium,
For now is fet the High Juftice:
And hath affignyd the day of Dome;

Kep

Repe you redyly to this grett assyse,
Both gret and small, all and sum,
And of your answer you now advise,
What you shall say when that yow com, &c.

These and such like, were the Plays which in
former Ages were presented publickly: Whe-
ther they had any settled and constant Houses, for
that purpose, does not appear; I suppose not. But
it is notorious, that in former times there was
hardly ever any Solemn Reception of Princes,
or Noble Persons, but Pageants (that is Stages
Erected in the open Street) were part of the
Entertainment. On which there were Speeches
by one or more Persons, in the nature of Scenes;
and besure one of the Speakers must be some
Saint of the same Name with the Party to whom
the Honour is intended. For instance, there
is an ancient Manuscript at *Coventry*, call'd
the *Old Leet Book*, wherein is set down in a
very particular manner, (fo. 168) the Reception of Queen *Margaret*, Wife of *H. 6*,
who came to *Coventry* (and I think, with
her, her young Son Prince *Edward*) on the
Feast of the Exaltation of the Holy-Cross, 35.
H. 6. (1456) Many Pageants and Speeches were
made for her Welcome; out of all which,
I shall observe but two or three, in the Old
English, as it is Recorded.

St.

St. *Edward*.

Moder of mekenes, Dame Margarete, princes moſt excellent,
I King Edward wellcome you with affection cordial,
Certefying to your highnes mekely myn entent,
For the wele of the King and you hertily pray I ſhall,
And for prince Edward my goſtly chylde, who I love principal.
Praying the, John Euangeliſt, my help therein to be,
On that condition right humbly I giue this Ring to the.

John Evangeliſt.

Holy Edward crowned king, Brother in Uerginity,
My power plainly I will prefer thy will to amplefy.
Moſt excellent princes of wymen mortal, your Bedeman will I be.
I know your Life ſo vertuous that God is pleaſed thereby
The birth of you unto this Reme ſhall cauſe great Melody:
The vertuous voice of Prince Edward ſhall dayly well encreaſe,
St. Edward his Godfader and I ſhall prey therefore doubtleſe.

St. *Margaret*.

Moſt notabul Princes of wymen earthle
Dame Margarete, the chefe myrth of this Empyre,
Ye be hertely welcome to this Cyte.
To the pleſure of your highneſſe I wyll ſet my deſyre;
Both nature and gentleneſſe doth me require,
Seth we be both of one name, to ſhew you kindneſſe;
Wherfore by my power ye ſhall haue no diſtreſſe.

I ſhall pray to the Prince that is endleſe
To ſocour you with ſolas of his high grace;
He will here my petition this is doubtleſſe,
For I wrought all my life that his will wace.
Therefore, Lady, when you be in any dredfull caſe,
Call on me boldly, thereof I pray you,
And truſt in me feythfully, I will do that may pay you.

In the next Reign (as appears in the ſame Book, fo. 221) an other Prince *Edward*, Son of

of King *Edward* the 4, came to *Coventry* on the
28 of *April*, 14 *E*. 4, (1474) and was entertain'd
with many Pageants and Speeches, among
which I fhall obferve only two; one was of
St. *Edward* again, who was then made to fpeak
thus,

Noble Prince Edward, my Coufin and my Knight,
And very Prince of our Line com yn diffent,
I Saint Edward habe purfued for your faders imperial Right,
Whereof he was excluded by full furious intent,
Unto this your Chamber as Prince full excellent
He be right welcome. Thanked be Crift of his fonde,
For that that was ours is now in your faders honde,

The other Speech was from St. *George*; and
thus faith the Book.

———Alfo upon the Condite in the Crofchep-
ing was St. George armed, and a kings daughter kneling afore him with a Lamb, and the fader
and the moder being in a Towre aboben behold-
ing St. George faving their daughter from the
Dragon, and the Condite renning wine in four
places, and Minftralcy of Organ playing, and
St. George hauing this Speech underwritten,

O mighty God our all fuccour celeftiall
Which this Royme hath given in dower
To thi moder, and to me George protection perpetuall
It to defend from enimps fer and here,
And as this mayden defended was here
By thy grace from this Dragons debour,
So, Lord preferve this noble prince, and ever be his fouour,

Lovew. I perceive thefe holy Matters confift-
ed very much of Praying; but I pitty poor St.
Edward the Confeffor, who in the compafs of a
few

few Years, was made to promise his favour and assistance to two young Princes of the same Name indeed, but of as different and opposite Interests as the two Poles. I know not how he could perform to both.

Trum. Alas! they were both unhappy, notwithstanding these fine Shews and seeming caresses of Fortune, being both murder'd, one by the Hand, the other by the procurement of *Rich.* Duke of *Glocester*. I will produce but one Example more of this sort of Action, or Representations, and that is of later time, and an Instance of much higher Nature than any yet mentioned, It was at the marriage of Prince *Arthur*, eldest Son of King *Henry* 7. to the Princess *Catherine* of *Spain*, *An.* 1501. Her passage through *London* was very magnificent, as I have read it described in an old M. S. Chronicle of that time. The Pageants and Speeches were many; the Persons represented St. *Catherine*, St. *Ursula*, a Senator, Noblesse, Virtue, an Angel, King *Alphonse*, *Job*, *Boetius*, &c. among others one is thus described, ——When this Spech was ended, she held on her way tyll she cam unto the Standard in Chepe, where was ordeyned the fifth Pagend made like an hevyn, theryn syttyng a Personage representing the fader of hevyn, beyng all formyd of Gold, and brennyng beffor his trone vii Candylis of war standyng in vii Candylstykis of Gold, the said personage beyng environed wyth sundry Gyrarchies off Angells, and syttyng in a Cope of most rich cloth of Tyssu, garnisshyd wyth stoon and perle in most sumptuous wyse. For again which said

said Pagend upon the sowth syde of the strete
stood at that tyme, in a hows wheryn that tyme
dwellyd William Geffrey habyrdasher, the king,
the Quene, my Lady the Kingys moder, my
Lord of Oxynfford, wyth many othir Lordys and
Ladys, and Perys of this Realm, wyth also
certayn Ambassadors of France lately sent from
the Frensh King: and so passyng the said Estatys,
eyther guyvyng to other due and convenyent Sa-
luts and Countenancs, so sone as hyr grace was
approchid unto the sayd Pagend, the fadyr began his Spech as folowyth.

Hanc veneram locum, septeno lumine septum.
Dignumque Arthuri *totidem Astra micant.*

I am begynyng and ende, that made ech creature
Oy sylfe, and for my sylfe, but man esspecially
Both male and female, made after myne aun fygure,
Whom I joyned togydyr in Matrimony
And that in Paradyse, declaring oppnly
That men shall weddyng in my Chyrch solempnize,
Fygurid and signifyed by the erthly Paradyze.

In thys my Chyrch I am allway recydent
As my chyeff tabernacle, and most chosyn place,
Among these goldyn Candylstikkis which represent
Oy Catholyk Chyrch, shynyng affor my face,
With lyght of feyth, wisdom, doctryne, and grace:
And mervelously eke enflamyd toward me
Wyth the extyngwible fyre of Charyte.

Wherefore my welbelovid dowgthyr Katharyn,
Syth I have made yow to myne awn semblance
In my Chyrch to be maried, and your noble Childryn
To regn in this land as in their enherytance,
Se that ye have me in special remembrance:
Love me and my Chyrch your spiritual modyr,
For ye dispysing that won, dyspyse that other.

Look

𝕷𝔬𝔬𝔨 that 𝔂𝔢 𝔴𝔞𝔩𝔨 in my 𝔭𝔯𝔢𝔠𝔢𝔭𝔱𝔰, and obey them 𝔴𝔢𝔩𝔩:
And here 𝕴 give 𝔶𝔬𝔴 the same 𝔟𝔩𝔢𝔰𝔰𝔦𝔫𝔤 that 𝕴
𝕲𝔞𝔳𝔢 my 𝔴𝔢𝔩𝔩 𝔟𝔢𝔩𝔬𝔳𝔢𝔡 𝔠𝔥𝔶𝔩𝔡𝔢𝔯 of 𝕴𝔰𝔯𝔞𝔢𝔩𝔩;
𝕭𝔩𝔢𝔰𝔰𝔶𝔡 be the 𝔣𝔯𝔲𝔶𝔱 of your 𝔟𝔢𝔩𝔶;
𝕻𝔬𝔴𝔢𝔯 𝔰𝔲𝔟𝔰𝔱𝔞𝔫𝔠𝔢 and 𝔣𝔯𝔲𝔱𝔶𝔰 𝕴 𝔰𝔥𝔞𝔩𝔩 𝔢𝔫𝔠𝔯𝔢𝔞𝔰𝔢 and 𝔪𝔲𝔩𝔱𝔶𝔭𝔩𝔶;
𝕻𝔬𝔴𝔢𝔯 𝔯𝔢𝔟𝔢𝔩𝔩𝔦𝔬𝔲𝔰 𝕰𝔫𝔦𝔪𝔶𝔢𝔰 𝕴 𝔰𝔥𝔞𝔩𝔩 put in 𝔶𝔬𝔴𝔯 𝔥𝔞𝔫𝔡,
𝕰𝔫𝔠𝔯𝔢𝔞𝔰𝔦𝔫𝔤 in honour both 𝔶𝔬𝔴 and 𝔶𝔬𝔴𝔯 𝔩𝔞𝔫𝔡.

Lovew. This would be cenſured now a days as profane to the higeſt degree.

Trum. No doubt on't: Yet you ſee there was a time when People were not ſo nicely cenſorious in theſe Matters, but were willing to take things in the beſt ſence; and then this was thought a noble Entertainment for the greateſt King in *Europe* (ſuch I eſteem King *H.* 7. at that time) and proper for that Day of mighty Joy and Triumph. And I muſt farther obſerve out of the Lord *Bacon*'s Hiſtory of *H.* 7. that the chief Man who had the care of that Days Proceedings was Biſhop *Fox,* a grave Counceclor for War or Peace, and alſo a good Surveyor of Works, and a good Maſter of Ceriṁonies. and it ſeems he approv'd it. The ſaid Lord *Bacon* tells us farther, That whoſoever had thoſe Toys in compiling, they were not altogether Pedantical.

Lovew. Theſe things however are far from that which we underſtand by the name of a Play.

Trum. It may be ſo; but theſe were the Plays of thoſe times. Afterwards in the Reign of K. *H.* 8. both the Subject and Form of theſe Plays began to alter, and have ſince varied more and

E   more

more. I have by me, a thing called *A merry Play betwene the Pardoner and the Frere, the Curate and Neybour Pratte.* Printed the 5 of *April* 1533. which was 24 *H.* 8. (a few Years before the Diſſolution of Monaſteries) The deſign of this Play was to redicule Friers and Pardoners. Of which I'll give you a taſte. To begin it, the Fryer enters with theſe Words,

> Deus hic; the holy Trynyte
> Preſerue all that uow here be.
> Dere bretherne, yf ye well conſyder,
> The Cauſe why I am com hyder,
> Ye wolde be glad to knowe my entent ;
> For I com not hyther for mony no₂ for rent,
> I com not hyther for meat no₂ for meale,
> But I com hyther for your Soules heale, &c.

After a long Preamble, he adreſſes himſelf to Preach, when the Pardoner enters with theſe Words,

> God and St. Leonarde ſend ye all his grace
> As many as ben aſſembled in this place, &c.

And makes a long Speech, ſhewing his Bulls and his Reliques, in order to ſell his Pardons for the raiſing ſome Money towards the rebuild-ing,

> Of the holy Chappell of ſweet ſaynt Leonarde
> Which late by fyre was deſtroyed and marde.

Both theſe ſpeaking together, with continual interruption, at laſt they fall together by the Ears. Here the Curate enters (for you muſt know the Scene lies in the Church)

Hold

Hold your hands; a vengeance on ye both two
That euer ye came hyther to make this ado,
To polute my Chyrche, &c.

Fri. Mayster Parson, I marvayll ye will giue Lycence
To this false knaue in this Audience
To publish his ragman rolles with lyes.
I desyred hym ywys more than ones or twyse
To hold hys peas tyll that I had done,
But he wolde here no more than the man in the mone.

Pard. Why sholde I suffre the more than thou me?
Mayster parson gaue me lycence befoze the.
And I wolde thou knowyest it I haue relykes here.
Other maner stuffe than thou dost bere:
I wyll edefy more with the syght of it,
Than will all thy pratynge of holy wryt;
For that except that the precher himselfe lyue well
His predycacyon wyll helpe neuer a dell, &c.

Parf. No moze of this wranglyng in my Chyrch:
I shrewe yowr hertys bothe for this lurche.
Is there any blood shed here between these knaues?
Thanked be god they had no staurs,
Nor egotoles, for then it had ben wronge.
Well, ye shall synge another songe.

Here he calls his Neighbour *Prat* the Constable, with design to apprehend 'em, and set 'em in the Stocks. But the Frier and Pardoner prove sturdy, and will not be stockt, but fall upon the poor Parson and Constable, and bang 'em both so well-favour'dly, that at last they are glad to let 'em go at liberty: And so the Farce ends with a drawn Battail. Such as this were the Plays of that Age, acted in Gentle-

E 2

mens

mens Halls at Chriftmafs, or fuch like feftival times, by the Servants of the Family, or Strowlers who went about and made it a Trade. It is not unlikely that * Lords in thofe days, and Perfons of eminent Quality, had their feveral Gangs of Players, as fome have now of Fidlers, to whom they give Cloaks and Badges. The firft Comedy that I have feen

* Till the 25 Year of Queen *Elizabeth*, the Queen had not any Players; but in that Year 12 of the beft of all thofe who belonged to feveral Lords, where chofen & fworn her Servants, as Grooms of the Chamber. Stow's *Annals*, p. 698.

that looks like regular, is *Gammer Gurton's Needle*, writ I think in the reign of King *Edward* 6. This is compofed of five Acts, the Scenes unbroken, and the unities of Time and Place duly obferved. It was acted at *Chrift* Colledge in *Cambridge*; there not being as yet any fettled and publick Theaters.

Lovew. I obferve, *Truman*, from what you have faid, that Plays in *England* had a beginning much like thofe of *Greece*, the Monologues and the Pageants drawn from place to place on Wheels, anfwer exactly to the Cart of *Thefpis*, and the Improvements have been by fuch little fteps and degrees as among the Ancients, till at laft, to ufe the Words of Sir *George Buck* (in his *Third Univerfity of* England) *Dramatick Poefy is fo lively expreft and reprefented upon the publick Stages and Theatres of this City, as* Rome *in the* Auge *(the higheft pitch) of her Pomp and Glory, never faw it better perfom'd, I mean (fays he) in*

refpect

respect of the Action and Art, and not of the Cost and Sumptiousness. This he writ about the Year 1631. But can you inform me *Truman*, when publick Theaters were first erected for this purpose in *London* ?

Trum. Not certainly; but I presume about the beginning of Queen *Elizabeths* Reign. For *Stow* in his Survey of *London* (which Book was first printed in the Year 1598) says, *Of late Years in place of these Stage-plays* (i.e. those of Religious Matters) *have been used Comedies, Tragedies, Interludes, and Histories, both true and feigned; for the acting whereof certain publick Places, as the Theatre, the Curtine, &c. have been erected.* And the continuator of *Stows* Annals, p.1004, says, That in Sixty Years before the publication of that Book (which was *An. Dom.* 1629) no less than 17 publick Stages, or common Playhouses, had been built in and about *London.* In which number he reckons five Inns or Common Osteries, to have been in his time turned into Playhouses, one Cock-pit, St. *Paul*'s singing School, one in the *Blackfriers,* one in the *Whitefriers,* and one in former time at *Newington* Buts; and adds, before the space of 60 Years past, I never knew, heard, or read, of any such Theaters, set Stages, or Playhouses, as have been purposely built within Man's Memory.

Lovew. After all, I have been told, that Stage-Plays are inconsistant with the Laws of this Kingdom, and Players made Rogues by Statute.

Trum.

Trum. He that told you so strain'd a point of Truth. I never met with any Law wholly to suppress them: Sometimes indeed they have been prohibited for a Season; as in times of *Lent*, general Mourning or publick Calamities, or upon other occasions, when the Government saw fit. Thus by Proclamation, 7 of *April*, in the first Year of Queen *Elizabeth*, Plays and Interludes were forbid till *Alhallow-tide* next following. *Hollinshed*, p. 1184. Some Statutes have been made for their Regulation or Reformation, not general suppression. By the Stat. 39 *Eliz.* c. 4. (which was made *for the suppressing of Rogues, Vagabonds and sturdy Beggars,* it is enacted, S. 2, **That all persons that be, or utter themselves to be, Proctors, Procurers, Patent gatherers, or Collectors for Goals, Prisons or Hospitals, or Fencers, Barewards, common players of Interludes and Minstrels, wandring abroad, (other than Players of Interludes belonging to any Baron of this Realm, or any other honourable Personage of greater Degree, to be authorized to play under the Hand and Seal of Arms of such Baron or Personage) All Jugglers, Tinkers, Pedlers and Petty chapmen, wandering abroad, all wandring Persons, &c. able in Body, using loytering, and refusing to work for such reasonable Wages as is commonly given, &c. These shall be ajudged and deemed Rogues, Vagabonds and sturdy Beggars, and punished as such.**

Lovew. But this priviledge of Authorifing or Licenfing, is taken away by the Stat. 1 *Ja.* 1. ch. 7. S. 1. and therefore all of them (as Mr. *Collier*

lier says) are without distinction brought under the foresaid **Penalty**.

Trum. If he means all *Players without distinction*, 'tis a great Mistake. For the 39th of the Queens Statute extends only to *Wandering Players*, and not to such as are the King or Queen's Servants, and establisht in settled Houses by Royal Authority. On such, the ill Character of vagrant Players (or as they are now called, Strolers) can cast no more aspersion, than the wandring Proctors, in the same Statute mentioned, on those of *Doctors-Commons.* By a Stat. made 3. *Ja.* 1. ch. 21. It was enacted, **That if any perſon ſhall in any Stage-play, Enterlude, Shew, Maygame oꝛ Pageant, jeſtingly oꝛ pꝛophanely ſpeak oꝛ uſe the holy name of God, Chꝛiſt Jeſus, the holy Ghoſt, oꝛ of the Trinity, he ſhall foꝛfeit foꝛ every ſuch offence,** 10 l. The Stat. 1. *Char.* 1. ch. 1. enacts, **That no Meetings, Aſſemblies, oꝛ concourſe of People ſhall be out of their own Pariſhes, on the Loꝛds day, foꝛ any Spoꝛts oꝛ Paſtimes whatſoever, noꝛ any Bear-bating, Bull-bating, Enterludes, Common Plays, oꝛ other unlawful Exerciſes and Paſtimes uſed by any perſon oꝛ perſons within their own Pariſhes.** Theſe are all the Statutes that I can think of relating to the Stage and Players; but nothing to ſuppreſs them totally, till the two Ordinances of the Long Parliament, one of the 22 of *October* 1647, the other of the 11 of *Feb.* 1647. By which all Stage-Plays and Interludes are abſolutely forbid ; the Stages, Seats, Galleries, &c. to be pulled down; all Players tho' calling themſelves the King or

Queens

Queens servants, and as such Acting within this Realm, all of them *on Conviction,* to be *punished and fin'd according* to Law; the *money forfeited by* them to go to the Poor of the Parish; and every Spectator to Pay 5 *s.* to the use of the Poor. Also Cock-fighting was prohibited by one of *Oliver*'s Acts of 31 *Mar.* 1654. But I suppose no body pretends these things to be Laws; I could say more on this Subject, but I must break off here, and leave you, *Lovewit*; my Occasions require it.

Love. Farewel, Old *Cavalier.*

Trum. 'Tis properly said; we are almost all of us, now, gone and forgoten.

F I N I S.

CPSIA information can be obtained at www.ICGtesting.com
Printed in the USA
LVOW05s1926080814

398220LV00017B/656/P